THE LITTLE BOOK OF GOOD HORSEMANSHIP

Elaine Heney

Copyright Elaine Heney Nov 23rd 2007.

All rights reserved.

Published by Irish Horsemanship, Nov 2007.

Printed in the U.S.A. 2nd edition, March 2008.

No part of this book may be reproduced or transmitted in any form or by any means, electronic or mechanical including photocopying, recording or by any information storage and retrieval system, without permission from the publisher in writing. The information in this book is true and complete to the best of our knowledge. All recommendations are made without any guarantee on the part of the publisher, who also disclaims any liability incurred in connection with the use of this data or specific details.

For further information, please visit:

www.irishhorsemanship.com

Visit our online horsemanship discussion group here:

http://irishnhsociety.proboards41.com/index.cgi

Many thanks to John & Margaret Heney.

Contents

1. Introduction .... - 1 -
2. Training horses and groundwork .... - 4 -
3. Words of wisdom .... - 13 -
4. Food .... - 18 -
5. Turnout and stabling .... - 21 -
6. Feet and farriers .... - 27 -
7. Management words of wisdom .... - 28 -
8. 'On the bit' the nice way .... - 30 -
9. Riding words of wisdom .... - 39 -
10. Solving problems .... - 42 -
11. My horse's behaviour has changed ...... - 44 -
12. Safety .... - 46 -
13. Should I buy a horse? .... - 49 -
14. Mature or young horse? .... - 55 -
15. I want a pony! .... - 62 -
Sample bill of sale - purchase agreement ... - 66 -

1. Introduction

Great horses have always been associated with great teachers and trainers. I believe that everyone has the potential to develop the skills needed to teach and train horses that you would be proud to call your own.

During my school days I wasn't very good at Irish. My knowledge was basic, and I found it hard to increase my vocabulary and get my head around all the tenses. The teacher's goal was to get us through the exams, any way she could. Even though most of us did pass the exams, I hated those classes with a passion. I would feel anxious, nervous and apprehensive before every single class. I dreaded each lesson, grew to dislike Irish immensely and I only learned because I was forced to. After I passed the final exam, I made a point of forgetting everything.

English classes were completely different. We had a brilliant teacher who taught us all we needed to know for the exams. As well as poetry and Shakespeare, she would regularly launch into tales of triumphs and disasters from the local political circles, recalling various larger than life characters. I looked forward to every class and by the end of the term had learned poetry, language, and a great appreciation for the art of story telling. She was a great teacher, and her students turned out pretty well too.

Sister Philomena was my piano teacher in Tipperary, and she instilled a love of music in me from an early age. To be a great pianist she believed that you needed three things - the head, the hands and the heart.

You needed to have a good head on your shoulders in order to learn and remember the pieces. You needed to have a good level of technical ability to play the correct keys at the correct time. And you needed your heart to make the music beautiful. The same goes for horses.

Firstly you need to know what to do, and the reasons for doing it – how to groom, tack up, feed, ride, etc. Then you need to be physically able and confident to do these things. So if you're feeling nervous or have a sore arm these things are a little more difficult. Lastly, from your heart comes softness and feel, fairness, kindness and willingness. All of these combine to create something beautiful.

My first pony was a cute short legged Shetland whose favourite pastimes were walking, stopping and eating. When I was six years old my riding instructor Mr. Dooley taught me two very important things.

- Gentle light hands which do not pull on a horse's mouth are worth their weight in gold.
- No one knows everything there is to know about horses.

There are two other important things I've picked up since then.

- The horse is always right.
- There is a reason for everything.

Horses are a never ending education. By using good horsemanship practices and being open to learning new and old ideas, you are well on your way to becoming a true horseperson.

2. Training horses and groundwork

A huge amount of a horse's potential and behaviour rests in the hands of its owner. Each moment you are with your horse – catching him, leading him into the yard, tacking up - you are in fact teaching him. If you are knowledgeable, kind, consistent and firm you can lay down boundaries and teach your horse good behaviour. Your horse will be a pleasure to be around.

If you don't know what you're doing or are aggressive, forceful, too laid back or don't insist on good manners, then you will more than likely end up with a horse who is aggressive, forceful, too laid back or has no manners.

If it's the horse who is in charge, then just like the lead horse in a herd, the horse will do what he wants, boss you about, etc. If there is something scary, your horse will take charge of the situation and bolt off if he feels it is necessary. If your horse doesn't want to leave the yard, then he'll refuse to go where you ask him to go as well. Your horse is now the boss and the boss makes the decisions. If he wants food, he'll push you out of the way to get it. He'll stand on your feet, walk into you, and generally do what he likes. If you allow him to be the boss, then your horse is within his rights to do this.

Get the groundwork right and the riding will follow.

A horse has the same perspective on life whether you are sitting in the saddle or walking along beside him. If your horse is happy and polite on the ground, he will usually be happy and polite in the saddle. If your horse is rude and barges on the ground you will often find he's not perfect when you are in the saddle either, and may refuse to walk on, be hard to stop or difficult to control.

If you can get the basic things right on the ground, then you will have a much nicer time when you are in the saddle. Here are a few basic things which are very useful to be able to do well on the ground.

Catching your horse.

When you open the stable door or walk towards your horse in the field your horse should turn his head around to face you. Be aware of your horse's perspective, as in order to receive respect you must also give it. Wait for a few seconds if needed until your horse turns around to acknowledge you of his own accord, then move closer towards your horse.

If your horse continues to ignore you make some noise or twirl a rope to catch his attention and ask him turn around towards you. Walking into a stable towards a horse's hindquarters is dangerous as you may get kicked. In a field you do not want to be walking towards a horse's hindquarters either. If your horse ignores you when he is in the field or starts to walk away from you as you approach, then make some noise and move your arms energetically to encourage him to walk further away from you. You want to catch a well behaved polite horse not a grumpy one. Keep asking your horse to walk or trot away from you, until you see him start to relax and think about being caught. It might take five seconds or it might take ten minutes. When your horse stands still quietly and looks at you, then walk up quietly and catch him.

Leading.

When leading use a loose lead rope. When you walk it's your horse's job to walk with you. When you stop it's your horse's job to stop exactly when you do. If your horse does this give them a rub.

If your horse keeps on walking or bumps into you, immediately ask your horse to take a step or two backwards.

Then when they are standing politely near you (but not too close) give them a rub as a 'thank you'. Then try it again. Keep the lead rein loose to allow your horse to make his own decisions.

Standing still.

Every horse should be able to stand still while you groom, mount, sit in the saddle, wash their tail, plait their mane or open a gate. These are basic but very useful requirements. If they can't stand still, try to figure out why. Are they sore or nervous, or are they confused about what you are asking them to do? What often works very well is to break one tricky thing down into a few easy things. Imagine you want to put a rug on your horse, but he's a bit nervous. Hold the rug near your horse, at a distance he feels comfortable with. If he turns his head to look at the rug or moves his nose a little closer to sniff the rug, immediately take the rug away from him as a reward. Give him a short rest then try again. Put the rug half an inch closer this time. If your horse walks away a little, keep the rug at the same distance and allow him to walk in a circle around you. The second he stops moving, take the rug away again as a reward. If he stands still with the rug a little nearer to him, also take the rug away as a reward. You are training your horse to stand still near the rug, but your horse actually thinks he is training the rug to move away from him by standing still.

Be polite and mannerly.

I am a big fan of nicely behaved horses. For example if you open their stable door your horse should stand in the stable quietly waiting until you invite him to walk out, rather than barge out past you. Your horse may be trained to always walk through gates between fields, rather than in a trot or canter (one day this may prove invaluable), be polite around you and other humans and to be easy to handle. Each one of these things you need to teach your horse. If your horse already knows these things, then you will just have to be vigilant and ensure that they retain these abilities. If you stop teaching, even a lovely horse can start to go backwards a little. That's why a great trainer can produce brilliant horses, but if that horse ends up in a home which doesn't have a good teacher, the horse can start to pick up small bad habits which can grow over time into larger bad habits. This is what you want to avoid so always try to be the best teacher you can be, whenever you are handling and riding your horse.

Riding preparations.

Before I ride, I always like to know my horse is well behaved, healthy and listening to me, and knows how to stop, start and turn.

If a horse is badly behaved on the ground, I'd like to fix those issues before I do anymore. It's safer than being bolted away with.

If my horse is well behaved on the ground, then I'm ready to tack up.

Touch all over.

Can you rub your horse all over (body, legs, head, ears, girth area)? Many riders have leaned back in the saddle and rested one hand on the hindquarters, and then ended up on the ground after a gigantic buck. Some horses can be nervous of a person standing near their hindquarters, or might not like people touching their ears. It's a great idea to have a horse which is comfortable with you, wherever you are and patient work on these areas can achieve a lot.

Confidence.

Stand beside your horse's shoulder. Very gently put a hand on his nose and ask him to bend his neck towards you a little. Also, as you stand at your horse's shoulder, you can pick up your lead rope and with a light contact ask your horse to turn his head towards you.

If your horse remains still and turns his head towards you even a little, that's great. If he keeps his body in a straight line and tries to avoid bending his neck by walking backwards, walk backwards with him and only stop asking when he stands quietly with a slight bend in his neck, and is relaxed. You are looking for flexion, softness and willingness.

To do this a horse needs to be supple and to have confidence and trust in you.

Asking a horse to stop.

To check that your horse understands the cues to slow down, stop and reverse, ask your horse lightly to move backwards by putting light pressure on a rein, or by lightly putting pressure with your fingers where the nose band would lie. If your horse starts to move his weight backwards, that's great. If he doesn't understand reverse, and either stands there looking at you or starts to walk into you, his brakes are likely to be a bit suspect.

Being able to reverse is the foundation for good brakes. If he looks at you with a puzzled expression, you might like to work on the brakes a little more on the ground before you disappear on horseback over the horizon.

Changing direction using a hindquarter yield.

A hindquarter yield, where the back legs move in a circle around the front legs, is a very useful manoeuvre for your horse to be able to perform. Stand beside your horse's back and ask your horse to turn his head a little around towards you. Now imagine where your heel would be, if your leg was a little behind the girth line. Very gently, touch this area with your finger as lightly as a fly, and then take your hand away. Ideally your horse will move one or two of his hind feet sideways away from you. This is good to change direction, to turn off the engine (power comes from the hindquarters) and improve suppleness. If this doesn't work, be patient, give your horse time, and try to make what you want him to do more obvious by using a gentle push to help him figure it out.

Changing direction and movement using a forequarter yield.

A good forequarter yield is essential for a horse to be able to perform, as without it you can have a horse with a very tense braced front end which makes moving correctly with softness and flexion much more difficult. Stand at the side of your horse's head. Look at his eye, and push his head away from you so he is looking where you will soon want him to go. Walk toward his head slowly, and tap the shoulder nearest you lightly and with a slow rhythm. Always give him a few seconds in between cues for him to have a think and figure out what you are asking him to do. The idea is that your horse will move his forequarters a step sideways away from you.

This is great to change direction while staying balanced when you are riding, to get weight off the forehand and to make sure your horse's shoulders are supple and free moving, which will give you a much nicer and more comfortable experience in the saddle. With your horse's strides being longer and more athletic your horse will cover ground more efficiently. If your horse plants his two front feet into the ground and braces his shoulders, it is advisable to do more work here before getting into the saddle.

3. Words of wisdom

- Be polite around your horse. Don't shout or run, don't make unexpected movements or use violence.

- Teach your horse to have good manners. A horse should not be allowed to walk over you. Having a horse that drags you around gets a bit frustrating after a while.

- Be fair. Only ask your horse to do what he is physically and mentally capable of. Don't ask your horse to do too much and lose his trust and confidence in you.

- Be consistent and don't move the goalposts. That makes life confusing and difficult to understand for your horse.

- Give your horse time and be patient. Don't expect instant results and don't expect your horse to get everything right first time. Be supportive and encourage everything they do right. Take care of your horse, because that's what matters to him.

- Be generous and willing. Work with your horse, rather than expecting him to work for you.

- Say thank you with a rub or a rest. If your horse has done a good job, make sure you tell him. Then he will know he's done a good job, and is more likely to repeat this behaviour.

- Handsome is as handsome does. It's not the packaging which counts, but the honesty, trust, courage and heart of the horse.

- To be successful there must be trust between horse and owner. Trust is earned over time and is of one of the most fundamental aspects of horsemanship.

- Good horsemanship rests on clear understandable communication between the horse and owner/rider. If your horse cannot understand your cues, there is little hope your horse will do what you want him to do. You are speaking two entirely different languages. This is quite a common issue. Ask yourself how you can become a better teacher.

- Reward every try, and keep your eyes open so you see when your horse tries.

When your horse is thinking what you are thinking (e.g. I want my horse to take a step back, and my horse starts to move his weight backwards) stop asking, release all pressure and give him a rub. Your horse will figure out what you want him to do quite quickly.

- Don't be afraid to ask for help. No one expects you to know everything.

- Safety always comes first. Horses and ponies can be dangerous and in extreme cases, can kill. Always be aware of safety issues and potential accidents and avoid them.

- Read as much as you can. Horses are more demanding than a master's degree, so you will need a lot of information in your head.

- Your horse knows more about horses than you ever will and you can learn a lot from him. If you can figure out your horse, his likes, dislikes, psychology and reasons for his behaviour, you are on the right path.

- Horsemanship isn't meant to be rocket science. If something sounds too difficult or harsh, maybe it is. There are lots of different ways to reach the same goals.

- Don't be afraid to make mistakes, just make sure you learn from them.

- Having a horse is meant to be hard work, but is also very rewarding, fun and enjoyable.

- If you treat a horse with respect and confidence he will mirror this back to you. If you treat a horse with aggression and temper, he will also mirror this back in his behaviour towards you.

- Leave temper and ego at the door. If it's a bad day do what you have to do and go home. It's not your horses fault. Chalk it up to experience and remember tomorrow is another day.

- If your horse doesn't understand something, work out how you can explain it more clearly and simply.

- Horses ask a lot of questions. Be prepared to listen to and answer all of them. Horses crave guidance and if you fail to respond you'll find habits developing that you don't like.

- The key to a truly successful partnership with the horse is respecting and understanding the emotions and instincts that govern every waking moment of his life.

- It's easier to train good behaviour into a horse than it is to train bad behaviour out of a horse.

- Some days will be so bad you'll wish you'd never met the beast, let alone bought it... but these are the days that will teach you most, and the ones you'll look back on with the fondest memories.

- Don't force a horse to do something. Give him a choice, and let him make his own decision. If he does the right thing, reward him with a rub or a rest.

- Always end on a good note. Horses remember a lot.

4. Food

Each horse has different needs, and based on where he lives will have different living quarters, including the availabilities of a stable, paddock or field.

Firstly a horse has to have adequate suitable food to keep him healthy and in good condition.

To begin, look at your horse and assess his current weight and health.

1. Is your horse in poor condition or does he look too skinny?

2. Does your horse look healthy, with his weight in proportion to his body for his breed and size?

3. Is your horse overweight?

Your horse's diet is something which will ideally be checked every few weeks, and be prepared to increase, decrease, add or subtract food as required in order to maintain your horse in good health.

The decrease in grass growth in autumn and winter will mean your horse is likely to need extra feed in the form of hay. Conversely the increase of new nutritious grass in spring will mean your horse will need to go into a smaller paddock, where he can't eat as much and so avoid getting over weight. Overweight horses can develop laminitis which can lead on to movement issues and can be fatal.

Secondly, you also need to look at what work your horse will be doing. If your horse is being ridden every day and you are preparing for competitions, your horse may need extra energy due to this extra workload. Extra energy can be added by increasing feed, again always keeping an eye on maintaining a healthy weight.

If your horse is doing a few rides a week, and is already in good condition just on grass or hay, don't be tempted to overfeed him. As you don't need any extra energy out of your horse, you don't need to put any extra energy (food) into your horse. Again, monitor your horse's weight and health condition every few weeks, and proceed from there. Horses can lose condition in just a few days, so do check your horse's condition every time you see him.

What type of food?

Grass is the natural diet for horses. They are designed to eat a little all day long. Forage such as grass and hay (dried grass) will keep your horse's digestive system in good health. Do not feed silage or grass cuttings from a lawnmower. Both can cause colic.

If your horse is doing a lot of work, or is underweight, you may look towards other types of food in addition to the basic grass / hay diet. If your horse is looking fine, has a healthy weight on just grass / hay, and has enough energy for the work you're currently doing with him, then he probably doesn't need any extra food. Each horse is different, so do consult someone knowledgeable in your area for specific advice on your own horse's needs.

Different types of horse foods can have different types of energy releasing qualities. Some food will have a quick effect and your horse will get a burst of energy. Other foods offer slower releasing energy, so it is useful to be aware of this and to feed for temperament. Talk to your feed supplier or local equestrian colleagues about what food would be best for your horse based on his work and competition requirements, current health and living arrangements.

5. Turnout and stabling

Turnout

Allowing a horse to spend time outside with other horses has many benefits.

Social engagement: Horses need social engagement and the company of other horses to keep them happy and feeling safe. It is common to see horses grooming each other, eating near each other and playing together. It's also great to teach horses basic manners.

Mental fitness: Horses need to have things to think about, and get bored being locked in a box all day. Being outside allows them to watch what is going on, investigate new things and keeps them mentally stimulated and happy. The opposite of this is an over-stabled horse which has developed stable vices.

Digestive health: Horses are built to eat a little grass, or other types of forage (hay, etc) all day long.

Physical fitness and health: No horse will get fit if they stand still all day. Horses develop muscle and keep themselves physically healthy by exercising themselves while they move around their paddock or field.

I would recommend that daily turnout is the minimum requirement for any healthy horse.

If you have your own land.

If you own or rent land then you may be able to allow your horse to live outside for part or all of each year. My three hunters (Irish sports horses) are lightly worked during winter and don't need to be clipped. They are well suited to living outside together without rugs in winter in Ireland, in secure fields with water, shelter and enough grass to keep them in good condition. Each autumn you will notice that your horse's coat (fur/body hair) will shed and he will start growing a thicker coat in preparation for winter. If you start using rugs this coat will not grow to be as warm/thick as it would naturally.

Older horses, horses with naturally thin coats (some thoroughbreds, warmbloods, etc), and horses which have been clipped may need a rug on, and this is something best researched by you as each horse will be different. Smaller stocky ponies, and native or stocky horses with thick furry coats may not need a rug on at all during winter.

During the winter, ideally your horse will need access to a larger field or paddock as the amount of grass will have decreased, and small areas tend to get muddy quickly.

It is also a good idea to divide your land up into a number of paddocks. While your horse is living in one paddock, your other paddocks are empty which gives the grass time to recover and grow again. This is common practise in traditional farming and grassland management. Assess your horse's condition and be prepared to make paddocks smaller in summer, larger in winter, and to feed extra hay in the winter if needed.

Continually assess your horse, his health and his requirements and ask for help and advice if needed always making sure your horse is looking happy and healthy.

I keep my horse at a livery yard.

Livery yards can offer grass livery, DIY livery, part livery or full livery.

If you don't have much time to visit and take care of your horse every day (it's not easy to balance everything) paying your livery yard to do the daily things like feeding, turnout or exercise is a useful solution.

Every day no matter what type of livery you choose, for a healthy body and mind your horse must have time outdoors to eat grass and interact with other horses. Horses are sociable animals designed to live in herds with other horses where they get social stimulation, exercise, learn manners and in essence learn how to be a horse.

If you choose full livery, ensure that it includes daily turnout. Horses were not designed to live full time in stables. When they are in the stable, you can add in some toys to keep them amused and give them something to do. Horses don't like being bored and may develop issues.

If your horse is doing a lot of work relative to the feed he is getting, look at increasing his feed ensuring he gets daily exercise and turnout. If your horse gets a day off, cut down his hard food for that day. If you give a stabled horse with no exercise and no access to grass a lot of hard food, even after just one day, you can cause something known as 'tying up', where the horse's muscles go into spasm, which is highly distressing for the horse. You will need to call a vet immediately.

Always feed your horse in relation to the work he is doing and include forage. Lack of forage (grass and hay) can cause serious veterinary issues including ulcers.

When a horse is in a stable they do not obviously have access to grass. Grass is the most natural and healthy food for a horse and so in its absence, hay is given. Horses do not eat three regular meals like humans. Instead, they keep eating a little, continuously all day long.

If you choose grass livery, make sure your horse has enough food in the winter (your horse will need a large paddock, and if he/she is losing weight, ensure an adequate daily supply of hay, haylage etc as appropriate). If you see your grass livery horse losing weight, talk to your yard owner straightaway and put a feeding regime in place which will ensure your horse stays healthy during the winter.

In the summer if your horse is on grass livery make sure he isn't getting too fat. Too much grass can cause problems. If your horse is becoming overweight arrange for him to be moved into a smaller paddock and keep an eye on him. Again, you want to maintain a healthy weight for the work your horse is doing, neither too thin or too overweight, both of which pose serious health risks.

With a horse on grass livery, you must check your horse's weight and overall health as regularly you would do a horse in full livery.

Livery yards and supplements.

Not all livery yards are equipped to feed individual horses according to requirements, so in some cases owners may need to provide specialist feeds or supplements required themselves.

I have an older horse, or a horse who finds it hard to keep on condition.

If you have an older horse, a bad-doer (a horse who finds it hard to put on weight) a horse who needs a carefully balanced and designed diet, or have certain items missing from your horse's current diet (e.g. natural mineral deficiencies in his grazing land), you may need to introduce some supplements and minerals into your horse's diet.

For all horses I would also recommend regular teeth checks. Older horses have older teeth, which can make eating more difficult. A loose tooth can actually drastically decrease how much a horse can eat and how much weight they can put on. Our thirty year old pony's front teeth are not great, so he can find it hard to eat short grass. So instead we have to make sure he always has longer grass available which he finds much easier to nibble.

Younger horses may also have teeth issues which can cause unwanted behaviour, loss of condition or health issues.

Feeding an older horse or a bad doer correctly is very important for their health and quality of life.

6. Feet and farriers

It is advisable to check and pick out your horse's feet every day. This allows you to examine for general wear and tear, check the state of your horse's shoes if he has some and to make sure the foot itself is healthy and without cracks. This only takes a minute or two. You can't ride a horse with a sore foot so it is in your interest to keep him sound.

It is good practise to get a qualified farrier out every six to eight weeks. If you see a crack in your horse's foot, get the farrier out straight away to sort it out. Small cracks can turn into big painful cracks. No foot, no horse.

To find your nearest fully qualified farrier, please contact your national farrier authority.

7. Management words of wisdom

- Every interaction with your horse is training and a learning experience for both of you.

- If it's not working, stop and work out why. There is no shame in changing your approach.

- Don't forget to enjoy your horse in between training and chores. There is always time for a scratch and rub.

- Make sure rugs are well fitted and comfortable. Take the rug off every day and check for injuries or rubbing.

- Think forage (grass and hay) and respect your horse's digestive system.

- Feed from the floor. Horses are designed to eat food from floor level, and feeding food from heights (haynets etc) can cause uneven wearing of the teeth which can lead to dental problems, and unwanted muscle development under your horse's neck. The correct feeding position aids respiration as the airways and the sinuses drain down and will also help the back muscles to develop correctly.

- Don't skip on the necessities. Horses need regular hoof care, teeth, worm management, back and saddle checks.

- Do what you believe to be true, right and fair. Do not rely on the professional being always right. Learn about horses and question all the time. If you don't like what you hear get a second opinion. It is your horse after all.

- When it is time to say goodbye let your horse go with love, comfort and with his dignity intact.

- Everyone appreciates being appreciated. Horses included.

- Never leave a horse out in a field or paddock with a nylon headcollar on. It can cause a lot of damage if it gets caught in something or if your horse manages to get it half off and it gets stuck. The safest way is to leave your horse outside without any headcollar on (you can train your horse to be easier to catch). If you MUST leave a headcollar on, make sure it is either a leather or field safe headcollar.

8. 'On the bit' the nice way

How can I get 'on the bit' nicely and easily with no gadgets, side-reins, double bridles or over bending and without needing arms of steel is a very common question.

'On the bit' isn't just one thing. It's actually lots of small things. When you put them all together then you get the rounded back, the engaged hindquarters, the vertical head flexion and the softness and suppleness and ease of movement that all come together under the 'on the bit' catchphrase.

The big question though before you begin, is **_why_** do you want to go on the bit?

Do you want your horse to look pretty? Do you want your horse to resemble a picture in a training book? Do you want to do it because people expect you to?

Or do you understand that to go 'on the bit' is really about developing an equestrian athlete who is physically prepared to be as successful as possible in your chosen equestrian pursuits?

Train your horse so he can do his job to the best of his ability while minimizing the risks of injury. Prepare him physically and mentally to be a top class athlete, whether you hack out with friends or compete internationally.

Your horse is an athlete.

To prepare an athlete you first need to make sure his whole body is soft, supple and flexible, and ready for your chosen equestrian discipline, whether it's western, hunting, jumping, dressage, polocrosse, etc.

Imagine your horse is a gymnast. Before every performance, a gymnast needs to warm up their muscles and make sure every part of their body is flexible. It's the same for horses.

For the best results when you are in competitions, riding for pleasure or practicing at home, first start by checking if your horse's body is soft and supple all over.

Can you move his head and neck on their own? Can you move just the back legs? Can you move just the front legs? Can your horse take a step back? Can your horse take a step forward? Can your horse take a step sideways? And can your horse do all of these things from the lightest of cues showing softness through his body, without any arguments, braces or tense muscles?

It may sound complicated, but all of these things are **the basics** any horse should be able to do before you go for a hack, compete in your local dressage competition or hit the road for the national showjumping championships in Dublin. And the good news is that they are all pretty easy to do.

I teach all of these on the ground first, but if you know how to teach them in the saddle that's fine too.

1. Lateral flexion – head and neck turned to one side - groundwork.

When riding on a circle, your horse's head and neck should follow the arc of the circle. You can practise this on the ground first to get it right by asking your horse to turn his head a little while he is standing still. Don't over bend, just ask for a little.

2. Hindquarter yield – groundwork.

A hindquarter yield involves moving the back legs in a circle around the front legs, which remain relatively still. Working properly on the bit means you need a soft flexible horse all over. The first thing you need to do is teach your horse to hindquarter yield on the ground. This also encourages the horse to step his hind legs under himself, similar to what you will be looking for soon. Hill work is also good to get the hind end engaged and working under the horse.

3. Forequarter yield – groundwork.

A forequarter yield involves moving the front legs in a circle around the hind legs, which remain relatively still. It is very good to loosen up your horses shoulders and take the weight of the forehand.

Imagine your horses back is long and straight like a dressage whip. Someone is standing in front of you holding both ends of the whip. You place your hand on the middle of the whip and press lightly downwards. The middle goes down, and both ends go up. If this was a horse, his head would be up, his shoulders would be tense and stuck, his back would be hollow, and his hindquarters wouldn't be under him.

Now look at that straight dressage whip again. Put your hand under the middle of it and press upwards. Now the middle is raised and the ends are lower. If this was a horse, his head would be down, his shoulders would be free moving and raised and his back rounded, and his hindquarters would be underneath him.

A horse which is tense or defensive or stiff will often have both front feet stuck into the ground. This means the shoulders will be braced and the head will be up. It will be very difficult to ask a horse like this to backup or to turn his front end.

If you can get the front end moving independently then the forelegs won't be stuck into the ground any more, the shoulders will free up and the back will be physically able to round. You'll also find you are getting much longer steps with the two front legs. Your horse will cover ground more economically (fewer strides) and it will be more comfortable for the rider.

4. Backup (reverse) – groundwork.

Backing up is a very good exercise to get weight off your horse's forehand, and is also very useful as part of training a horse that very light pressure on the reins means slow down. Like the forequarter yield, if your horse's shoulders are braced or locked you'll see this immediately when you ask them to take a step backwards from a light cue.

5. Sidepass and soft ribs – groundwork.

The sidepass is when the horse walks sideways. You get this by doing the hindquarter yield and the forequarter yield at the same time. The sidepass is very important. Your horse needs to start to understand that a little pressure with one leg while you're riding means that he needs to wrap his ribs around that leg.

Often times when you start doing this with a horse, if you put on one leg your horse will start to go faster without bending his body. Instead we need to train your horse that while light pressure from your two legs do indeed mean 'go faster', light pressure with just one leg means 'go sideways'.

So when you're circling if you want to go from a walk to a trot, put on two legs briefly until you're in trot. Then take them off again as its your horse's job to maintain this gait, not yours. Then when you want that bend in his body like the circle, just put on your inside leg lightly and your horse will stay at the same pace, but gently arc his ribs around your inside leg.

This is also known as 'soft ribs', and is **crucial** to be able to do in order to work towards 'on the bit'. Lateral flexion (bend in the neck) plus soft ribs (bend through the rest of the body) performed together, is the final step you do before going on the bit.

6. Repetition.

Repeat these in the saddle, until each is good, soft and easy on both reins. Conformation plays a small part but every horse has potential.

7. 'On the bit'.

To be able to go 'on the bit' as it's known locally, all of the things above need to have been done already. You should now be riding a horse who you can hindquarter yield, forequarter yield, backup lightly, sidepass, and circle on both reins with his full body (from poll to dock) arced in the same way as that circle. In the beginning you can work on very small circles. If you can do a small circle, the big circles will be easy.

The next step is teaching your horse how you want him to carry his head. Soft ribs and lateral flexion equals vertical flexion. To work on this walk your horse in a circle, maybe 10 or 15 metres.

Because of your inside leg, his ribs are soft (practise your sidepassing), causing him to arc around your inside leg from shoulder to hindquarter.

Your inside hand is gently asking for his head and neck to turn towards the inside. Your outside leg and hand do nothing at all.

There is a light contact on the inside rein as you maintain that inside flexion. Every now and again your horse will reposition his head either up or down slightly as he moves around. If your horse repositions it upwards, just keep that little bit of tension in the inside rein. If he repositions it downwards, loosen that inside rein completely. You are rewarding this behaviour with an immediate release of pressure.

You are teaching your horse that if he lowers his head a little, you are going to loosen that rein. If he keeps it where it is, or puts his head up, that rein is going to stay as it is. Remember, this is all just done in the walk. You'll end up really concentrating waiting for the next split second when he gives his head a little. It's actually quite fun!

Once your horse has started to figure this out, you can refine it a little and only release the rein totally when his head is lowered, and his nose is perpendicular to the ground. At the beginning it's a great idea to have a friend watching who can tell you each time he does it, as it can be difficult to see it from the saddle if you're not used to how it feels.

8. The final result.

Your horse's shoulders are free, so his back is able to round and you have lovely athletic long strides.

Working on the circle, his body is arced around your inside leg, and his head and neck are flexed slightly inwards.

Your horse has started to figure out that if he drops his head a little and brings his nose in a bit, that you release pressure on the inside rein (you're not using the outside rein at all). Now he is inclined to do this by himself, dropping his head in, rounding his back, and his hindquarters have started coming in under him a lot more than before.

From your perspective, light pressure with your inside leg automatically results in an arced horse. A light cue from you on the inside rein will result in your horse adjusting his head position to where you want, which is followed immediately by a release of pressure by you on that inside rein. When your horse comes down 'on the bit', you've actually got no weight at all in your hands.

While I say 'on the bit' you can actually do all of these things bitless. Keep it simple and you'll have a relaxed, balanced, supple, soft horse who floats over the ground.

9. Riding words of wisdom

- Start with the basics. When you stand beside your horse with just a head collar on him, can you move him lightly backwards (brakes), forwards, move his back legs sideways on their own and move his front legs sideways on their own (steering)? It's nice to know these are all working before you hop into the saddle.

- When you ride, if you feel relaxed, soft and supple, chances are your horse probably will too. If your body is tense and stiff when you are riding, your horse is probably tense and stiff too.

- If you're not having fun then your horse probably isn't either. You need to change what you are doing.

- Use light hands. Imagine your reins are two pieces of thread. The two reins are not the brakes. They are subtle communication tools.

- Ask nicely and give your horse a chance to respond, rather than expecting instant results. Horses aren't machines.

- If your horse is lame, do not ride until he or she is completely recovered. You could do more damage. No foot, no horse.

- 'On the bit' does not mean pull your horses head in hard or saw on the reins. If you do, you just get sore arms and end up with a horse with a tough mouth and a stiff front end. It means something entirely different.

- Don't kick your horse to ask him to move. If you are at a riding school and the horses have gotten used to being kicked and now ignore all riders legs (they are correct to do so as this is what they have been taught), and your teacher is advising you to kick, I'd suggest finding a different horse. Kicking a horse is not teaching you how to ride. It's teaching you how not to ride.

- Your teacher should teach you something new in every lesson. If they don't, find another teacher.

- Turn one big complicated thing into lots of simple small things. It makes teaching and learning a lot easier.

- If your horse has confidence problems, look to yourself - are you helping or hindering?

- When you're buying a bridle, buy what you need, not what looks sophisticated. Avoid trendy nosebands and big bits. It is not about looking 'up to date' it's about having nice, comfortable, simple equipment for your horse to help him to do the things you want him to do. All horses are born beautiful anyway.

- If your horse leans or is difficult to stop, retraining work on the ground using backup and reversing works really well. Once you've mastered this, then sit in the saddle and practice halt to backup, then walk to halt to backup, trot to walk to halt to backup, and then finally canter to trot to walk to halt to backup.

- People who constantly repeat the same things all the time run the risk of being ignored. If you would like your horse to do something, (e.g. walk on) ask him politely (e.g. little squeeze with both legs). When he walks on, then stop asking him to walk on (stop squeezing). If you squeeze all the time, including when your horse is already doing what you want him to do, you might be training your horse to ignore you.

10. Solving problems

From time to time, horses can develop quirks and display behavioural tendencies which are not wanted by its owner or rider. Here are some thoughts to keep in mind.

Your horse has a valid reason for everything that he does. A horse doesn't wake up one day and decide to buck. He bucks because there is something causing him to buck.

Find out what is causing the problem.

Instead of getting fed up with your horse and not knowing what to do, put on your detectives cap and spectacles and start to figure out what could be causing the problem.

There are a million and one reasons for a horse's behaviour. Here are a few common things to check:

1. Poor eyesight, sore back, mineral deficiencies, pain, sore feet, sore teeth, issues with bones or muscles, etc. A full veterinary check is always a good place to start. You never know what your vet might discover.

2. Badly-fitting tack. Bridles, bits and saddles which don't fit properly are not uncommon, and can cause your horse pain which can result in unwanted behaviour.

3. Too much energy going in and not enough space to let the energy out. Feed a horse a lot of hard food and keep him in a stable and you'll soon have a four legged rocket on your hands.

4. Incorrect handling. Even one hour of incorrect teaching can leave you with a horse with a problem. If you see your horse getting stressed, ask for advice about what you are doing. Ideally people and horses should be able to work quietly and happily together. It's not meant to be a battle. If it is, think about doing something differently.

5. The horse has learned that he can be the boss. This isn't a great idea. Ideally the human is the boss. Not a dictator – but an understanding, responsible, caring owner who the horse trusts and respects. If a horse hasn't got manners when you are on the ground, his manners when you are in the saddle probably aren't great either.

11. My horse's behaviour has changed

A horse's behaviour can change for many reasons. Often the only way a horse can tell you that something is wrong is by changing their behaviour. If they could explain it to us in English it would make things a lot simpler, but unfortunately that won't happen.

What kind of things can cause a horse's behaviour to change?

- Bolting can be caused by too much food, not enough exercise, sore teeth, sore back, pain, badly fitting tack, lack of leadership, etc.

- Bucking can be caused by badly fitting tack, pain, too much food, not enough exercise, sore teeth, lack of leadership, sore back, etc.

- Bad brakes can be caused by mis-training, a lack of training, sore mouth, sore teeth, badly fitting bit and tack, and pain anywhere though the horses body, amongst other things.

- A badly mannered horse can be created due to bad training, lack of training, too much food, not enough exercise, rough handling, no manners being taught at all, lack of leadership, pain, fear, etc.

- A horse may not load into a box because they are scared of what people will do to them when they approach the box (shout at them, hit them), they may be nervous walking into dark spaces, they may have had painful experiences near or in the box previously, there may be a lack of trust, there may be a lack of leadership, etc.

- Headshaking may be caused by sore teeth, sore mouth, badly fitting/painful bit, feet issues, rider influence, allergies, misalignment of the poll, bad saddle fitting, neurological issues, etc.

- A horse may kick the stable door because he's stabled for too long and doesn't have enough turnout (very important to check this), is hungry, sees everyone else getting fed before him, has learnt that kicking results in either food or attention, etc.

Your horse has a reason for everything that he does. Figure out the reason and you are in a much better position to begin to solve the problem. If you can put yourself in your horse's shoes you will be able to see a lot more clearly.

12. Safety

Always stay safe. Horses can be unpredictable and dangerous. If you feel uncomfortable at any time, ask yourself *'what would make me feel safer?'*

In an ideal world all horses would be mannerly, well trained and have sweet temperaments but this world is far from ideal. When I deal with a behavioural problem, I firstly take off the gadgets, look past the symptoms and try to figure out what is the cause of the problem.

If you are not a trainer or not very experienced with horses, gadgets can be useful as a very short term solution if they directly increase the level of safety for you, your horse, and the people and surroundings nearby. Your first responsibility as a horse owner is to keep everyone and everything safe.

If you need help with an issue, enlist the advice of a good horseperson you admire in your area to help you out. It works much better if you can fix the cause of the problem, not just mask the symptom.

One common problem with horses is bad brakes. Some horses are easy to stop, and some are not. This can happen for various reasons. Most tack shops have an assortment of exotic bits and nosebands which can look quite appealing for the horse owner who is tired of trying to get his horse to stop. Do what you need to keep everyone safe, but at the same time, don't settle for second best. Buying a more severe bit to improve your brakes might only mask the issue temporarily. When you take the new bit out, the problem may still be there.

There are ways to retrain your horse nicely to have light brakes and a talented horse trainer who understands the theories of groundwork, light pressure and release, and rewarding the try should be able to help. Check there are no dentistry or veterinary issues and then find someone who can help you and your horse to solve this specific issue.

It's not all about money.

You don't have to buy the most expensive things. The true judge of horsemanship is a happy, well mannered, well trained horse, not a wild thing you can't load who is dressed in €250 pink and purple travel rugs with matching boots. Looking the part will not get you that far with horses. They don't impress as easily as humans.

The most important word in horsemanship is 'why'.

You might know 'how' to do something. But more importantly you need to know 'why' you are doing it. You 'can' make fifty cups of tea, but 'why' do it if there's no one around to drink them? Horses are similar. Have a reason for what you do. Don't just follow the crowd. The crowd isn't always right. Follow your horse instead.

13. Should I buy a horse?

Deciding to buy a horse is a life changing decision - not only for you but also for your potential new horse.

Buying a horse is a dream for many people, but the reality can bring you down to earth with a crash. Literally.

Buying a horse is not like buying anything else.

If you are starting to play the piano you can go ahead and buy the most expensive beautiful sounding grand piano in the world and be completely safe and happy playing it to the best of your ability.

If you are a normal driver, proficient in the basics and can get from Cork to Dublin without crashing, you can go out a buy a beautiful Lamborghini convertible, and still be safe driving it within your ability obeying the speed limits and the rules of the road.

It you are a novice rider and you buy a very expensive, beautiful and well bred shiny competition horse you may however experience problems. As you do not know how to take care of this super horse, behavioural issues may develop which could lead to the horse misbehaving or getting confused and losing confidence. A few bad experiences will cause you to lose your confidence too. If you're nervous when you ride, this sensitive performance horse will pick up every movement and thought and will start to mirror your lack of confidence, spooking, behaving unexpectedly and you may fall off and get hurt. You could end up sore and scared with an expensive four-legged mistake who is confused, going backwards, labelled dangerous and back up for sale.

Louise.

Louise had started riding a few weeks ago and looked forward to her half hour lesson each Saturday immensely. She had 'bonded' with her riding school horse, and had spent hours relating all her horsey exploits to her work colleagues who listened patiently, though to be honest they were getting a bit fed up. During her riding lesson today she had attempted a trot on her own, and she was doing a nice impression of a sack of potatoes bouncing happily along. She walked up to the yard owner after her lesson, with a huge smile on her face.

"Hello, I've had about seven or eight lessons already and I would really love to buy my own

horse. Does it really cost that much to buy one and look after it?"

Louise wants the dream. But because her knowledge of horses and horsemanship is pretty limited, she has absolutely no idea about the millions of things she doesn't know. While her heart is in the right place, buying a horse is likely to be a disaster waiting to happen.

You have a responsibility to any horse you own to be the best owner you can be. For Louise, this would mean a few more years of lessons, gaining practical experience of handling horses, attending lessons and clinics, reading as many books as she could find, putting together a financial plan, and doing everything she can to become a more confident and knowledgeable horseperson.

John.

John has been riding for five years, and has done some show jumping and cross country competitions. He's got good ability, and has been helping out for the last two years with his friend's horse which he exercises three times a week. He has also got good horse sense, knows what's involved and has a sensible financial perspective. He has a number of equestrian friends whom he can ask for advice and help when he needs it. John knows that owning a horse is more than a dream. It's a full time job. John is in a good position to look for his own horse, and is hoping to get a sensible all rounder who he can learn more on and do some local and regional competitions.

Sally.

Sally has been riding for twenty years. She grew up on a farm with horses, went through pony clubs, hunted, hunter trialled, competed and won in university, worked in yards in Australia and has a beloved all rounder gelding who's done everything. She has helped out people starting horses, and now wants to buy a young unbroken horse to bring on herself. She has the experience, ability, horsemanship, equestrian help if needed, and time to turn both a quiet or more challenging youngster (you can buy either) into a success.

Cost.

Owning a horse will cost you a lot in hard cash, time, work, effort, daily checks, vet and farrier bills, sleepless nights, frustration, joy, more bills and hardship. The cheapest part of having a horse is the initial cost of buying it. You'll get used to trudging through muddy and windswept fields, mucking out dirty stables instead of sitting in front of a nice fire watching the football or your favourite soap. Your nails will become indescribable and your wardrobe will take a dramatic turn for the worse. You will fall off, probably hurt something, and at the very least develop a cowboy style gait which creates its own challenges in high heels. A peculiar odour will linger around you and in your car. This is the good stuff.

A horse needs to be checked every day (so much for that weekend away) and needs to be outside for all or part of each day. Holidays will be rare, due to lack of time, money and energy.

When you buy a horse, you are taking responsibility for its life. That is an incredible responsibility.

Ask yourself the following questions:

- Can I provide a happy healthy home for a half ton animal with a mind of his own? A horse is not a child, he is not a pet, he is not a human and he is not a toy. Do not treat him like one.

- Can I be the type of owner and trainer who makes a positive difference in the life of my horse?

- Do I have the time to look after a horse every single day?

- If I have a problem (sick horse, dangerous behaviour, unable to visit horse daily, need lessons, horsebox breaks down on motorway, etc) do I have friends and reliable horse people I can call upon for help and advice?

A good potential horse owner can answer yes to all of these questions.

14. Mature or young horse?

It all depends on who you are. There are always exceptions, but here are some general guidelines.

Mature horses.

Older horses have seen a bit more of the world, can be more forgiving and on average don't jump around as much as a green youngster. Also they're fairly settled in themselves so they are able to give you confidence and forgive your mistakes. 'Mature' is anything over 15 years. My mid twenties cob is still a lovely quiet but responsive ride, she competed when younger and still loves to jump and clears everything. Horses like this are worth their weight in gold.

Behind so many international competition riders is a story of how they learnt to ride on a sensible, plain, woolly, much loved horse or pony. This horse didn't move too quickly and didn't have much show potential. But he was honest and quiet, taught them all the basics, kept them safe, gave them confidence and a love of horses.

If you are looking for a first horse or pony, a horse like this of a suitable height and build for the jockey (child or adult), is a great idea.

If you've had a first horse or pony and have grown in confidence and ability then you're in a great position to look for something with a bit more jump and speed to bring you on to the next level, now that your riding is already quite skilled and you have buckets of confidence. Remember to buy what you need, not just something to look good.

A mature horse can offer a rider so much, and still look just as pretty as the young ones. Buying a young horse and 'learning together' is a big challenge for someone who's only been riding a few years.

You should also be aware that some older horses may have long established bad or dangerous habits and can be quite difficult, expensive and time consuming to fix, if at all for a novice rider.

Young horses.

If you're been around horses for a long time and know a fair bit, a young horse will be an exciting challenge. They need a confident quiet understanding teacher who doesn't mind a few unauthorised hops and jumps. The teacher needs to know exactly what they're doing.

Young horses ask a lot of questions. Bringing on a youngster well is one of the most enjoyable things you can do as an experienced horse owner and trainer. An experienced trainer can avoid any bad habits and vices, and end up with a potentially superb competition horse.

Young horses that have had a lot of work done when they are 2, 3 and 4 years of age may have been pushed too far too young, and this can result in health issues – bad backs, legs, etc. A horse is only physically mature somewhere between the ages of 5½ and 9 years of age. The bigger the horse, the longer he will take to mature. Excess work done before this age can cause health issues. The last parts of a horse to mature are his vertebrae/back bone. A lot of sharp turns, ridden work or fast work can cause physical issues. If you are buying a young horse which has been started or broken do ask what age they were started, and bear this information in mind.

If you feel out of depth with your young horse and would like help to bring him or her on, visit people in your area who start horses, and see how they work with a young horse and how skilled they are. Be aware that the word 'professional' doesn't always imply a lot.

Ask for telephone numbers of other clients for feedback, get references and watch how they start other horses. If you decide to get an experienced horseperson to 'make' your horse, if possible be present for most of your horse's training sessions. You will learn a lot.

Horses which are five or six years of age are still young horses, and still learning themselves. They will mature and blossom with a knowledgeable and understanding teacher in the saddle.

The perfect fit.

No matter what horse you buy, he or she has to be the right horse for you. You will need to consider the following:

1. **Size:** You should feel comfortable and relaxed riding your horse, and your horse should be tall and broad enough for him to be able to carry you comfortably. So much of good riding ability is about confidence. Does your horse give you confidence when you are on board?

2. **Good conformation:** Good conformation which is in reality good physical engineering, will reduce the chances of veterinary issues and should lead to nice movement.

3. **Good movement:** Good movement is very important with a horse or pony. Ideally you'd like your time in the saddle to be comfortable, so a horse who has an easy gait and covers ground economically is usually more appealing

than one which has a short staccato gait with legs going like the clappers.

4. **Full veterinary check:** Find out if your horse is physically sound, or has any underlying medical issues which may affect his behaviour, performance and resale value.

5. **Temperament and performance:** Experienced horse owners, equestrian professionals and horse trainers can often retrain horses with issues successfully. If you do not train horses professionally you are better off buying a horse which is easy to handle and already has good manners. It just makes life a lot simpler and more enjoyable. No one likes getting run away with or being trampled over by a scared or nervous horse.

6. **Your performance:** What can you do as a rider? If you are jumping small courses locally, buy a horse who can also jump small courses nicely. It doesn't make sense to buy a point to point racehorse who is a regular on the national circuit and jumps houses for fun, or a national winning eventer with bloodlines back to ancient times, just to gallop around a one foot high riding school course. It would be like driving that Lamborghini with hyper sensitive steering, turbo charged speed and a backseat full of unexpected surprises. You could end up in tears, draped over the sorry remains of a small multi-cross-pole.

7. **Colour:** Colour is not important. A good horse is never a bad colour.

8. **Cost**. An expensive horse does not mean that he is more suited to you than a less expensive horse might be. His ability and temperament must be suited to your ability and goals. But also a cheap horse is normally cheap for a reason. Find out what the reason is, how that reason will affect you riding and handling him, and then make your decision.

In the horse world it is always buyer beware.

When buying a horse don't believe a word you hear or read. This includes newspaper adverts, internet adverts, etc. Believe only what you see standing in front of you. Watch the horse closely, bring an experienced person with you, look for guarantees, ask for a trial, use a purchase agreement, get receipts for deposits and payments, and always get your potential new horse examined by a veterinary surgeon with experience of horses.

Sometimes a great rider and a great horse just don't gel into a good team. If you have initial reservations, go with your gut instinct. Ask yourself if you feel safe and confident on this horse, and if you feel you can give the horse the confidence he/she needs. Sometimes everything can look fine on paper, but there is a little voice in your head that is worried. Follow your instinct.

If you are interested in a horse, it is a good idea to get a trial of the horse for a few days before you decide, and then vet.

Buying horses is easy. Buying the right horse is very difficult.

At the end of this book there is a sample bill of sale - purchase agreement which is recommended to have when buying a horse.

15. I want a pony!

When you are buying the most treasured of creatures, the young riders 'first pony' (whether the rider is five or fifteen), it is not what the pony looks like which is important. The following two questions are what really matter.

1. Is the pony well mannered and well trained, and will he or she keep your young rider safe in the equestrian activities they will do?

    For example, if you have a 'lead reiner' rider, buy a pony which is quiet on the lead rein. If you have a novice pony clubber, buy a pony or small horse who can quietly complete a one day event with good manners and honesty.

2. Will the pony increase your young rider's confidence?

    Confidence is so important with horses. A suitable horse or pony will make its rider feel confident every time they ride him. If your rider feels scared on their pony it will never work.

An ideal first pony will be suitable in size for the child in question. Do not buy your child a large pony they will 'grow into'.

Buy a pony your child will be capable of handling and riding confidently. Also do not give your child a whip, unless you have a very good reason. Teach them good horsemanship instead.

A small, medium or large pony which is quiet, well trained, sensible and honest, and matches the skills of the young rider is the ultimate first pony.

As the young rider grows taller, in a few years they might start to look a bit big on their first pony. At this stage, they might now be trotting and cantering on their own, doing small jumps and pony club activities. It is now time to look for a slightly bigger and more competitive pony.

A second pony should also keep the young rider safe, and continue to improve their confidence.

Again, do not buy a very big pony in the hope that your child will grow into it. This is called 'over-horsing' and is not a good idea. You do not want a young rider to lose their confidence.

- The most important aspect is that the new pony will suit the child's ability.

- Buy a pony your child can handle and ride now, and hopefully enjoy for the next few years.

- Even a nervous rider will do brilliantly on a quiet slower pony, and you will see them smiling as their pony yet again brings them home safely.

- A confident showjumper who has been riding for a few years will however get fed up on a quiet pony and will want something suitable which jumps instead.

An important note to the parents and guardians.

Pretending your novice rider is actually a confident showjumper is very dangerous. The first responsibility of a parent or guardian is to keep the child in your care safe and healthy. Do not 'over horse' your child as they can quickly end up in hospital.

Also, you must assume that you will be the person who does all of the hard work - mucking out, grooming, catching, feeding, management, finding help, dealing with tantrums (pony or child!) wiping away tears, paying bills, handling, veterinary care, driving horses boxes, bringing the young rider to lessons, buying associated paraphernalia, cancelling holidays for pony camps, etc.

As with horses, buying a pony is easy but buying the right one is very difficult. But get the mix right, and your young rider and his or her pony will have years of fun and enjoyment together.

I WISH YOU AND YOUR HORSES MANY YEARS OF FUN, ENJOYMENT AND REWARDING HORSEMANSHIP. IF YOU WOULD LIKE TO LEARN MORE, YOU ARE VERY WELCOME TO VISIT US ONLINE:

www.irishhorsemanship.com

Elaine Heney, Irish Horsemanship Nov 2007.

Elaine is also the author of the 'Gentle Horsemanship for Young Riders' cdrom.

++++++++++++++++++++

A great horse has a great teacher.

Sample bill of sale - purchase agreement

By kind permission of

Ecklands Sports Horses, Dublin.

www.ecklandssportshorses.com

Seller details : _____

Buyer details: _____

Name _____

Address _____

Telephone _____

1. This agreement is made between _____herein referred to as the buyer and _____ herein referred to as the Seller.

2. Horse to be purchased:

Horse's name: _____

Sex:_____

Colour: _____

Registered Yes/No

If Yes, Registered No. is_____

3. Consideration

In consideration of the total sum of €_____,

SELLER agrees to sell and BUYER agrees to buy the said horse described above on the terms and conditions further set forth herein.

4. Payment Terms

The purchase is for cash and BUYER agrees to pay €___First Payment Amount___ as Deposit / Full Settlement on the _12_____ day of ___August__, 20

_ _/_ _/20 _ _ Amount in euros € _____

Any additional payment are recorded here

_ _/_ _/20 _ _ Amount in euros €_____

_ _/_ _/20 _ _ Amount in euros €_____

and, BUYER further agrees to pay the balance due of €_Final Payment___ on or before the _____ day of _____, 20_ _.

If purchase price is to be paid in instalments the terms shall be:

A down payment in the sum of _____First Payment_____ is due on the _____Date_____. The monthly payments shall be in the amount of ___Monthly Payments Agreed_____ and will be due and payable on the ___Day___day of each month for _No of Months_____months.

The registration papers if recorded above will be surrendered to the buyer at the time the last payment is made.

If horse is being purchased on a contract sale, _____ (seller) does require/does not require an insurance policy showing seller as loss payee.

Name of Insurance Company _____
Policy # _____.

If the said horse dies or becomes permanently disabled without insurance coverage, the buyer agrees to complete contract in full. The horse in a contract sale will be kept at this address _____ until paid for in full. The buyer is responsible for all stabling, grazing, farrier and veterinary costs and any other incidental bills pertaining to said horse. The buyer agrees to give seller thirty (30) days notice in writing if the said horse is to be moved.

The Buyer agrees to surrender the horse within 7 days of default on any payment under this agreement and the buyer is considered in default of this agreement as described at 8 below.

5. Registration and Ownership Transfers

Upon confirmation of payment in full as set forth above, SELLER agrees to promptly execute all necessary papers and to take all necessary steps to transfer ownership and registration of the animal to BUYER at no cost to the BUYER.

6. Warranties

(1) The SELLER warrants s/he has clear title to said horse;

(2) The SELLER makes no other warranties, express or implied, including the warranties of fitness for a particular purpose except as may be otherwise provided for in this Agreement as in (3) below;

(3) The SELLER warrants the following:

EG: Fully Sound, Novice Ride, No Vices etc _____

_____
_____
_____
_____

(4) BUYER warrants that BUYER has had the option to review the condition and health of the horse, prior to delivery or collection including any veterinarian examinations, at BUYER's expense.

(5) In the event said horse shall not meet any of the above warranties at the time of delivery, provided same is discovered within 7 days from the date of delivery to BUYER, SELLER agrees to do the following:

<u>Accept return of the horse</u>

<u>Return in full all monies paid for the horse</u>

7. Risk of Loss

(1) On completion of this agreement the BUYER shall assume the risk of loss of said horse

8. Buy back option

_____ *(seller) does wish/does not wish to retain the right to buy the above horse back if the new owner(s) decide to sell. This first right of refusal is valid until ____/_____/20 for a price not to exceed €_____.*

9. Default

If the buyer is unable to fulfill the contract, the horse will be returned to the seller in satisfactory condition. The sale will be nullified and all previous payments made will be forfeited. The buyer agrees that the seller have full entitlement to enter onto the premises or property where the horse is been held in order to recover the animal.Upon material breach of this Agreement by one party the other party shall have the option to terminate same.

10. Captions and Headings.

Any captions or headings used in this Agreement are for descriptive purposes only and are not to be considered terms of this Agreement.

Executed this _____ day of _____, 20 _ _

Buyer: _____

Seller :_____

For and on behalf of _____ (seller).